KINGFISHER
READERS

2

Trucks

Brenda Stones and
Thea Feldman

KINGFISHER
NEW YORK

Copyright © Kingfisher 2013
Published in the United States by Kingfisher,
175 Fifth Ave., New York, NY 10010
Kingfisher is an imprint of Macmillan Children's Books, London.
All rights reserved.

Distributed in the U.S. and Canada by Macmillan,
175 Fifth Ave., New York, NY 10010

Library of Congress Cataloging-in-Publication data
has been applied for.

Series editor: Thea Feldman
Literacy consultant: Ellie Costa, Bank Street College, New York

ISBN: 978-0-7534-6960-6 (HB)
ISBN: 978-0-7534-6927-9 (PB)

Kingfisher books are available for special promotions
and premiums. For details contact: Special Markets
Department, Macmillan, 175 Fifth Ave., New York, NY 10010.

For more information, please visit
www.kingfisherbooks.com

Printed in China
9 8 7 6 5 4 3 2 1
1TR/1012/WKT/UG/105MA

Picture credits
The Publisher would like to thank the following for permission to reproduce their material. Every care has
been taken to trace copyright holders. However, if there have been unintentional omissions or failure to trace
copyright holders, we apologize and will, if informed, endeavor to make corrections in any future edition.
Top = t; Bottom = b; Center = c; Left = l; Right = r
Cover Shutterstock (SS)/Konstantin Sutyagin; Pages 4-5 SS/Fernando Rodrigues; 6 SS/Christina Richards;
7t Bob Langrish; 7b SS/Cathleen A. Clapper; 8 SS/Sergio Schnitzler; 9t Shutterstock/Steve Estvanik;
9b Photolibrary/HBSS HBSS; 10t Shutterstock/Stephen Mahar; 10-11 SS/Robert Pernell; 11 Corbis/Alvis
Upitis/AgStock Images; 12 SS/R. Carner; 12-13 SS/Michail Kabaovitch; 14 SS/Orientaly; 15 SS/Orientaly;
16 SS/abutyrin; 17 Photolibrary/Imagebroker; 18 SS/Dimitry Kalinovsky; 19 SS/Stephen Mcsweeny; 20
SS/Marafona; 21 SS/Marafona; 22t SS/Bram van Broekhoven; 22b SS/Florin C.; 23 SS/Sergey Kozoderov;
24 Photolibrary/Tom Brakefield; 25t SS/Daniel Goodchild; 25b Photolibrary/Peter Robinson; 26 SS/Mike Brake;
27 SS/Mike Brake; 28 SS/Alexander Chelmodeev; 29 SS/GTibbetts; 30–31 Alamy/Don Hammond/Design Pics
Inc.; 31 SS/mashe

Contents

Here come trucks

This big truck has a job to do!

It carries a **load** from place to place.

A load is anything carried by a truck.

Other trucks are hard at work too.

Let's take a look!

Moving trucks

This moving truck
is filling up
with a family's things.

It will carry the whole load
to a new house.

Some trucks even move animals.

These horses
can rest and
enjoy the ride.
Neigh!

Heavy movers

Some trucks move very heavy things.

This truck carries a lot of new cars.

Each car weighs thousands of pounds!

This truck **hauls** hundreds of large logs out of the forest.

A forklift moves many heavy boxes at one time.

Tanker trucks

Tanker trucks carry liquids such as oil or water.

Tanker trucks are long and round.

This tanker will be filled with fresh milk!

On the road

Trucks can travel a long way.

Out on the road,
a truck driver sits
in the **cab** of a truck
and drives for hours.

Sometimes a truck is
on the road for days.

Sometimes a driver pulls over
and sleeps in the cab!

Farm trucks

Trucks on farms do big jobs to make life easier for farmers.

A **tractor** truck pulls a **plow** that makes rows in the ground where a farmer will plant seeds.

This combine harvester helps a farmer when plants are ready to be picked.

It cuts plants out of the ground and takes them apart very quickly.

The wheel deal

Some trucks have special wheels.
And some trucks have no wheels!

Big, strong wheels help this truck
carry its heavy load of coal.

Instead of wheels, metal belts move this truck easily over soft ground.

Construction trucks

Many kinds of trucks work
at a **construction site**.

A digger's claw digs up the ground.

A bulldozer pushes the soil
out of the way.

It clears the area
so construction can begin.

A dump truck carries soil
and rocks away from the site.

The back of the truck lifts,
and the load falls out.

A **concrete** mixer mixes
a batch of concrete
in its barrel.

Concrete is used
at many
building sites.

This truck has a crane.

The crane lifts things
to the top of a building
under construction.

Trucks in town

There are a lot of trucks
at work in your town.

Here are some you may see.

A road sweeper cleans the streets.

A garbage truck picks up trash.

This truck
takes away
trash that
can be
recycled.

Fire trucks

This fire truck is working at a fire!

The fire truck has hoses, ladders, and many other things needed to put out the fire.

Working the roads

Make way for the steamroller!

It flattens the **asphalt**
for a new road.

This snowplow moves snow
off the road
so that cars and trucks
can drive safely.

Trucks on the go

This truck is a lot like the one at the start of this book.

It's on the road with its load!

What do you think it is carrying?

A lot of trucks are hard at work.

Which one do you like best?

Glossary

asphalt a mix of sand, gravel, and other things that is used to make the top of a new road

cab the part of a truck where the driver sits

concrete a mixture that hardens to become a strong building material

construction site a place where things, such as buildings, are built

hauls moves something big and heavy from one place to another

load anything carried by a truck

plow a heavy farming tool with blades that make rows in soil for planting seeds

recycled used again

tractor a truck used on a farm for pulling heavy things such as a plow